Cultural Traditions in
Argentina

Adrianna
Morganelli

Crabtree Publishing Company
www.crabtreebooks.com

Crabtree Publishing Company

www.crabtreebooks.com

Author: Adrianna Morganelli

Publishing plan research and development:
Reagan Miller

Editorial director: Kathy Middleton

Editors: Janine Deschenes, Crystal Sikkens

Proofreader and indexer: Petrice Custance

Photo research: Crystal Sikkens

Designer: Tammy McGarr

Production coordinator and prepress technician:
Tammy McGarr

Print coordinator: Katherine Berti

Cover: Puppet in window of home in La Boca neighborhood in Buenos Aires (top left); Argentine vineyard (top); Flowering tree of erythrina crista-galli (top right); Bandoneon (bottom right); Andean tapestry (bottom center); Yerba mate in calabash gourd with bombilla (bottom left); Empanadas (bottom left); National Congress building, Buenos Aires (background); Couple dancing the tango (center)

Title page: Young performer celebrating Carnival in Salta, Argentina

Photographs:
Alamy: © imageBROKER: pp 8, 19;
© ONTHEBIKE.PL: pp 30–31 (bottom)
AP Images: NATACHA PISARENKO: pp 10,12, 13 (top);
Creative Commons: p7 (middle); Pablo D. Flores: p 14;
virginiainnocenti: p18; Liam Quinn: p24; Horacio Cambeiro: p25;
Gonzalo Rivero: p30 (left)
iStock: © IS_ImageSource: p5; © Grafissimo: p6;
© RnDmS: pp 20 (bottom), 21
Keystone: © Patricio Murphy: p11;
© E]Martin Zabala pp16–17 (bottom);
Public Domain: Horaciogris: p9; Bruno Girin: p13 (bottom);
José Lazarte: p17 (top right); Claudio Elias: p27
Shutterstock: © Kobby Dagan: cover (dancers);
© Michel Piccaya: title page; © Elena Mirage: p4 (bottom);
© Matyas Rehak: p20 (top); © sunsinger: pp 22, 23;
© T photography pp 26, 28–29 (bottom);
Thinkstock: mychadre77: cover (middle right)

All other images by Shutterstock

Library and Archives Canada Cataloguing in Publication

Morganelli, Adrianna, 1979-, author
     Cultural traditions in Argentina / Adrianna Morganelli.

(Cultural traditions in my world)
Includes index.
Issued in print and electronic formats.
ISBN 978-0-7787-8086-1 (bound).--ISBN 978-0-7787-8090-8 (paperback).--
ISBN 978-1-4271-8100-8 (html)

     1. Festivals--Argentina--Juvenile literature. 2. Holidays--Argentina--
Juvenile literature. 3. Argentina--Social life and customs--Juvenile
literature. 4. Argentina--Civilization--Juvenile literature. I. Title.
II. Series: Cultural traditions in my world

GT4831.A2M67 2016   j394.26982   C2015-907455-X
                                                                      C2015-907456-8

Library of Congress Cataloging-in-Publication Data

Names: Morganelli, Adrianna, 1979- author.
Title: Cultural traditions in Argentina / Adrianna Morganelli.
Description: New York : Crabtree Publishing, [2016] | Series: Cultural
     traditions in my world | Includes index. | Description based on print
     version record and CIP data provided by publisher; resource not viewed.
Identifiers: LCCN 2015047438 (print) | LCCN 2015045744 (ebook) |
     ISBN 9781427181008 (electronic HTML) |
     ISBN 9780778780861 (reinforced library   binding : alk. paper) |
     ISBN 9780778780908 (pbk. : alk. paper)
Subjects: LCSH: Festivals--Argentina--Juvenile literature. | Holidays--
     Argentina--Juvenile literature. | Argentina--Social life and customs--
     Juvenile literature.
Classification: LCC GT4831.A2 (print) | LCC GT4831.A2 M67 2016 (ebook) |
     DDC 394.26982--dc23
LC record available at http://lccn.loc.gov/2015047438

Crabtree Publishing Company

www.crabtreebooks.com   1-800-387-7650

Printed in Canada/022016/IH20151223

Published in Canada
Crabtree Publishing
616 Welland Ave.
St. Catharines, ON
L2M 5V6

Published in the United States
Crabtree Publishing
PMB 59051
350 Fifth Avenue, 59th Floor
New York, New York 10118

Published in the United Kingdom
Crabtree Publishing
Maritime House
Basin Road North, Hove
BN41 1WR

Published in Australia
Crabtree Publishing
3 Charles Street
Coburg North
VIC 3058

Contents

Welcome to Argentina!

Argentina is a country located in South America. It is the largest Spanish-speaking country in the world. Its celebrations and customs are influenced by the many different cultures and ethnic groups that live there. Many people have **immigrated** to Argentina from European countries including France, Italy, Germany, Ireland, and the United Kingdom.

Over three million people live in Buenos Aires, the capital city of Argentina.

4

Most Argentines are Roman Catholic, which is a branch of the **Christian** religion. Many of the country's holidays and festivals are based on their beliefs. There are a few other religions practiced in Argentina as well. Argentina has the largest Muslim community in all of Latin America. Muslims practice the religion of Islam, which is based on the teachings of the prophet Muhammad. About two percent of Argentina's population practices the religion of **Judaism.**

Did You Know?
In Argentina, lunch is the largest meal of the day. Some workplaces close for lunch so workers can spend it with their families.

Lunches are often so big that dinner is not eaten until 9:00 p.m.!

The New Year

Argentines celebrate the New Year, or *Ano Nuevo*, on January 1. On New Year's Eve, families and friends share a late dinner of traditional foods, which often includes *sandwiches de miga*. These are sandwiches made on white bread without the crust, and are filled with vegetables and thinly sliced meat. Just before midnight, people leave their homes to join the fun of the many street parties.

Argentines dance, sing, light firecrackers, and watch firework shows.

Turron is a popular New Year's dessert. It is a nougat made with honey, sugar, egg white, and nuts such as toasted almonds.

Piononos, which are pastry rolls filled with fruit or cream, are often enjoyed by Argentines on New Year's Eve.

On New Year's Day, many people attend church services to pray for a peaceful new year. In the afternoon, families often celebrate by swimming and picnicking on the many beaches along the Atlantic Coast. People also gather with family and friends for a special New Year's Day meal.

Carnaval

Carnaval is one of the largest fun-filled celebrations in Argentina. It takes place two weeks before Lent, which is the traditional period of **fasting** before Easter for Roman Catholics. People dress in colorful costumes and gather in the streets to dance, sing, and participate in parades. Many parades also include large, elaborate floats.

Argentina's largest Carnaval celebration takes place in the town of Gualeguaychú.

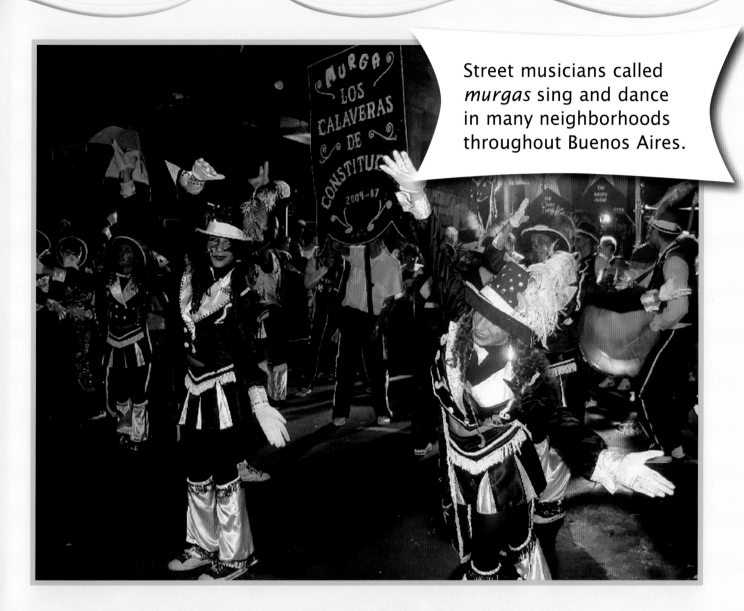

Street musicians called *murgas* sing and dance in many neighborhoods throughout Buenos Aires.

Each region of Argentina celebrates Carnaval in a different way. In Salta, the streets are filled with people dancing traditional South American dances known as the samba and *carnavalito*. In the northeast, people sing Argentine folk songs called *chamamé* accompanied by accordions and harps.

Did You Know?
During Carnaval, children play many water games, including throwing balloons and emptied eggshells filled with water.

Easter

Easter is a favorite celebration shared among Argentine family and friends. Many Argentines attend church services called masses and **processions** during the week before Easter known as *Semana Santa*, or Holy Week. On Good Friday, Christians are reminded of Jesus's **crucifixion** on the cross.

On Good Friday, many Argentines watch reenactments of Jesus's final hours as he carried the cross to his crucifixion.

Bakers in Buenos Aires made the longest loaf of Easter bread ever baked in South America. It measured 492 feet (150 meters) long, and took three weeks to make!

Easter Sunday is the day Christians celebrate Jesus's resurrection, or rising from the dead. Many families gather for an *asado*, or traditional Argentine barbecue of lamb and other meats. People share a special cake called *Rosca de Pascua*, which is baked in the shape of a ring to represent eternal life. After the Easter meal, people exchange eggs with family members and friends. Children's Easter egg hunts are also organized throughout many cities in Argentina.

May Revolution

Argentines show their **patriotism** by **commemorating** the date in 1810 when Argentina's first local government was established. Each year on May 25, Argentina celebrates *La Revolucion de Mayo*, or the May Revolution.

During May Revolution activities, children wave their country's flag as they parade behind a man dressed as an Argentine soldier.

Argentines dress in traditional *gaucho* costumes and dance in the streets in celebration of their country's independence.

People gather on the May Revolution holiday to listen to speeches by government officials and to sing Argentina's national anthem. Argentines enjoy music, parades, and food such as *locro*, a stew served with a hot sauce called *quiquirimichi*.

The May Pyramid is a commemorative monument in the main square in Buenos Aires known as the *Plaza de Mayo*.

National Flag Day

Each year on June 20, Argentines celebrate *Dia de la Bandera Nacional*, or National Flag Day. This holiday commemorates the country's flag, as well as the death of Manuel Belgrano, who designed the flag. The festivities include military parades and speeches. Argentina's president attends the celebration.

Did You Know?
The sun featured on Argentina's flag is a replica, or copy, of an engraving on the country's first coin.

On *Dia de la Bandera Nacional* people carry a giant version of their country's flag through the city's streets.

A monument called the National Flag Memorial was built in the city of Rosario, in 1957. Ceremonies are held at the monument throughout the day on this holiday. Across Argentina, a special pledge to the country is recited to students.

A monument of Manuel Belgrano stands in the Plaza de Mayo Square, in Buenos Aires.

Tango Festival

The world's largest tango festival is held in Argentina. The tango is a traditional form of Argentine dance that is performed by partners. Tango dancing is a major part of the country's culture. The Tango Buenos Aires Festival is held for more than two weeks every August. The festival includes a nine-day celebration of tango shows. More than half a million visitors attend the festival each year.

The Tango Buenos Aires Festival features tango performances to live orchestras held in ballrooms throughout Buenos Aires.

The festival begins with a huge *milonga*, or dance, where thousands of tango dancers called *tangueros* dance in the city streets.

Many tango competitions are held during the Tango Buenos Aires Festival. The winners receive special prizes and are invited to perform at future tango festivals. For people who do not know how to dance the tango, famous tango teachers offer free classes. This way, everyone is able to join in the party!

Did You Know?
Tango originated along the Rio de la Plata, or River Plate, which is an **estuary** that borders Argentina and Uruguay.

Oktoberfest

Although this is a traditional German event, the Oktoberfest festival in Argentina is one of the world's largest celebrations. The two-week celebration begins on October 10 each year. Thousands of people travel to the mountain village of Villa General Belgrano, in Cordoba, where German **immigrants** first celebrated Oktoberfest in the 1960s.

Thousands of Argentines and tourists enjoy the Oktoberfest every year.

Men and boys often wear traditional German knee-length shorts with suspenders called *lederhosen*, while women and girls wear colorful dresses called *dirndls*.

Oktoberfest is also known as the Beer Festival. Beer is an adult drink made from a grain called barley. Throughout the festival, people sample locally made beer, while enjoying traditional German foods, such as Bratwurst sausage. Dancers, orchestras, and people dressed in traditional German costumes parade through the streets. Each year a new *Reina del Oktoberfest*, or Oktoberfest queen, is chosen.

Day of Tradition

Each year on November 10, Argentines celebrate *Dia de la Tradicion*, or Day of Tradition. On this day, people celebrate the birth of an Argentine *gaucho* named José Hernández. Hernández wrote a famous poem called "El gaucho Martín Fierro" about the hardships of the *gauchos* in Argentina.

Gauchos live in the lowlands, or Pampas, of South America. They herd livestock and cattle year-round on ranches called *estancia*.

Many different horse-riding events take place throughout Argentina on *Dia de la Tradicion*.

In towns and cities across Argentina, people celebrate *Dia de la Tradicion* with parades, **rodeos**, and concerts. Men dress in traditional *gaucho* clothing and display their horse-riding abilities in various contests. Vendors offer traditional Argentine foods, such as *asado*, meat pies called *empanadas*, and an herbal drink called *mate*.

23

Christmas

Christmas in Argentina takes place during the country's summer season. On Christmas Eve, families gather for a late dinner at nine o'clock in the evening. After the meal, people dance, sing, and enjoy fireworks displays. At midnight, Argentine children open the gifts brought to them by Papa Noel, or Father Christmas. Families then attend midnight mass.

Children are able to visit Papa Noel at many shopping malls during the Christmas season.

On Christmas Day, many people in Argentina attend church services throughout the day. Some people sing Christmas carols door to door within their neighborhoods. Families gather for a feast, which is usually eaten outside.

Did You Know?
Three Kings Day is celebrated in Argentina on January 6. The night before, children leave their shoes outside or beneath the Christmas tree to be filled with gifts from the three kings, or Magi. Hay and water are also left for the Magi's horses.

Almost every home in Argentina is decorated with a *crèche*, or **nativity** scene.

Vitel toné is a traditional Christmas food. It is cold, sliced veal covered in a tuna-flavored sauce.

Food Festivals

Sharing meals is a way for families to spend time together. Because of this, food has become an important part of Argentine culture. Throughout Argentina, many festivals are held to celebrate the country's traditional foods.

Asado is meat that is usually cooked over an open fire, and it is commonly found at Argentine festivals and celebrations.

An enormous apple monument stands in General Roca to commemorate the region's most produced fruit.

National Apple Festival

The *Fiesta Nacional de la Manazana*, or National Apple Festival, is held every February in the city of General Roca, in Rio Negro province. This region produces the most apples in Argentina. During the festival, contests are held for the biggest and heaviest apple.

Grape Harvest Festival

In the province of Mendoza, a grape harvest festival called *La Fiesta de la Vendimia* takes place for three days in March. Thousands of people gather to celebrate wine and the winemaking industry. The grapes are blessed on the vines to ensure a good year's harvest. People enjoy parades and fireworks shows, and sing and dance to traditional folk music.

During *La Fiesta de la Vendimia*, 18 *reinas*, or queens, are chosen from each of the areas that make up the Mendoza province. The women then parade through the streets on floats.

National Yerba Mate Festival

Argentina's national drink, *mate*, is celebrated at the *Fiesta Nacional de la Yerba Mate*, or National Yerba Mate Festival. It is held each year in July in Apostoles, Misiones. *Mate* is a traditional South American drink made by steeping the dried leaves of the yerba mate plant in hot water. The drink is poured into a hollowed **calabash gourd**, and served with a metal straw called a *bombilla*.

29

National Tamale Festival

La Fiesta Nacional del Tamal, or National Tamale Festival, is held every July in the city of Salta to celebrate the tamale. Tamales are a traditional Argentine food made with a corn-based dough. They are wrapped in corn husks or banana leaves, then stuffed with meats, cheese, vegetables, or fruit. The festival features traditional gaucho folk music, dancing, and Argentine *asado*, or barbecue.

The tamale is one of Argentina's favorite foods!

National Empanada Festival

One of the most popular foods in Argentina is the empanada, a baked or fried pastry stuffed with meat, eggs, and vegetables. It is the favorite street food of Argentines, and is often served at parties and feasts. Every September, the province of Tucumán hosts the National Empanada Festival. Visitors to the festival sample the Tucumanian empanada, which is stuffed with beef and cooked in a fat-filled tray.

Most empanadas are cooked in a clay or gas oven.

Glossary

calabash gourd The fruit of the calabash tree

Christian The religion based on the teachings of Jesus Christ

commemorate To honor

crucifixion The death of Jesus upon the cross

estuary An area where the river flows into the sea

fast To abstain from eating food

immigrate To move to a new habitat or place

Judaism The religion, philosophy, and culture of Jewish people

nativity The birth of Jesus Christ

patriotism The love and defense of one's country

procession A group of people walking in a ceremonial manner

rodeo A public exhibition that showcases riding and cowboy skills

Index